A WORSHIP HANDBOOK

SPONSORS AND BAPTISM

Elaine Ramshaw

AUGSBURG FORTRESS / MINNEAPOLIS

CONTENTS

BAPTISMAL SPONSORS 3

WHAT'S A GODPARENT TO DO? 5

BEFORE AND DURING THE BAPTISM 7

PARTICIPATING IN YOUR GODCHILD'S ONGOING FAITH JOURNEY . . . 9

SPONSORING AN ADULT 13

APPENDIX A: Notes on the Baptism 15

APPENDIX B: Additional Resources 16

Sponsors and Baptism: A Worship Handbook
Copyright © 2002 Augsburg Fortress. All rights reserved. Except brief quotations in critical articles or reviews, no part of this book may be reproduced in any manner without prior written permission from the publisher. Write to: Permissions, Augsburg Fortress, Box 1209, Minneapolis, MN 55440-1209.

Book design: Richard Krogstad
Cover art: Jane Pitz
Editors: Robert Buckley Farlee, Rebecca Lowe

Manufactured in the U.S.A.   ISBN 0-8066-4295-5
08 07 06 05 04 03 02 01   1 2 3 4 5 6 7 8 9 10

Baptismal Sponsors

Being a Christian isn't something that one can do in isolation. When Jesus called people to follow him, one at a time or several at once, he was inviting them into community. Thus, the Bible tells of the twelve disciples who were closest to Christ, and of the larger numbers of people who gathered around Jesus whenever possible. After Jesus' death and resurrection, his followers continued to form communities of prayer and meal-sharing and mutual support. In Acts and in the apostolic letters, there are glimpses of these sorts of gatherings in the homes of people like Lydia (Acts 16) and Priscilla and Aquila (Acts 18; Romans 16). These local congregations of diverse believers became themselves signs of the whole Body of Christ, the communion of all the believers.

This, then, is basic to the Christian faith: to be Christian is to be in community. One way the church has lived out this truth is to arrange for persons being baptized to have sponsors who will accompany them in their faith journey. These sponsors have had different sorts of ongoing relationships with the ones they sponsor in different times and places in the history of the church. Consistently, though, they have been a sign and vehicle of the larger community's care for the one being baptized. When adults were baptized in the early church, sponsors vouched for their character and accompanied them through the long process of becoming a part of the Christian community. Babies and small children didn't need character witnesses, but they did need someone to speak the baptismal promises for them and take responsibility for those promises until the child matured. In the first centuries of the church's life, a small child was usually sponsored by a parent. By the beginning of the sixth century, however, persons other than the parents were being given that role.

It is not known why this shift in practice from parent-sponsors occurred. There is no record of any bishop or council advising that the change be made. Only centuries after the custom was established would there be a rule enforcing it. Parents themselves may have begun the practice of asking other adults to act as sponsor for their children, perhaps as a way to honor their friends and to ensure their interest in the child's welfare. At any rate, Christian families were enlarged by adding godparents, as parents recognized that every baby would need more than just its own family to help it grow up in the faith.

Today Christians still have sponsors for everyone being baptized, whether they are babies, children or adults. *Lutheran Book of Worship* uses the word "sponsor" because that word works no matter what the age of the person being baptized. A sponsor for a baby or small child is often called a "godparent," and that can be a better word to use in explaining to children who you are, as it's a much more intriguing word to a child. It also gives you a way of naming the child in relation to you: You're my godchild!

What's a Godparent to Do?

This book will mostly address being godparent to children, since that is the most common age for baptism in the Lutheran church. At the end of this booklet you will find some thoughts relating to sponsoring someone who is baptized as an adult.

There are two main parts to the job description of a godparent. First, you are to speak for the child who is not old enough to speak for herself or himself, answering the baptismal questions with the words of the creed on the child's behalf. Second, you are to be a spiritual friend and mentor to the child as he or she grows up and throughout his or her life. The essence of this two-part job description has remained the same since at least the sixth century among all churches that have had godparents.

Because the church hopes that each child baptized will come to claim the community's faith as her or his own, you as godparent are asked to be a spiritual mentor to your godchild, to support that growth into faith. This is the concern of the question in the baptismal rite that is answered by the parents and sponsors together (*LBW*, p. 121, #6). Some of the concrete things mentioned in that question may be done by the parents or by the child's congregation and not directly by you. When you answer "I do," you are promising to support the child's family as they bring up the child in the faith, but you are also promising to provide spiritual nurture for the child yourself. There is no one right way to do this; how you do it will depends on your personality and your godchild's, on your godchild's family's practice of the faith, on familial and cultural traditions of godparenting in your heritage. This booklet will make suggestions for ways you can live out the role of godparent, and you will need to try them on for size and adopt (or adapt) what fits for you and this particular godchild.

Godparental responsibilities other than the two spiritual duties listed above are largely a matter of ethnic cultural traditions. Among some Hispanic Americans, the godparent is expected to co-parent the child, helping to raise him or her, perhaps disciplining as a parent would. Some African Americans take godparenting very seriously as a way of making kin, so that godparents might, for instance, assume financial responsibility for the child. As long as these godparental roles support and enhance the basic role of spiritual mentorship, the church affirms and encourages them.

One question that often comes up is whether godparents are expected to raise the child if the parents die. That has been true at some places and times in the past, and it may be assumed in some ethnic cultures today. The current American legal situation, however, is that godparenthood as such has no legal status with regard to issues of guardianship. If the parents want to designate someone to take care of their children if they themselves die, they need to name that person as the legal guardian in their will.

Before and During the Baptism

Some godparents live near their godchildren; some do not. Some congregations have developed the helpful practice of choosing a sponsor (either the primary godparent or a supplemental one) from within the congregation as a way of helping to assure the child's ongoing connection to that congregation. In any case, if you live near your godchild's family, you will probably be able to participate in the baptismal preparation sessions that the pastor usually holds with parents or other family members bringing the child for baptism. These sessions will give you a chance to explore with the child's family and pastor the meaning of baptism and the nature of your role as sponsor.

During these sessions or outside of them, it would be a good idea to talk with the child's family about what shape your relationship with the child might take over time. What are the expectations or hopes about what that relationship could be? How might one best be a godparent in this particular family, this particular congregation, with these particular cultural traditions of godparenting? You might want to covenant with the child's family, promising them to stay connected with their child.

There may be things you can make or provide for the baptism itself. You could make or decorate or buy the baptismal candle that is lit from the paschal candle and given to the person being baptized, a candle which can be lit in later years on the anniversary of the baptism. Some congregations or families have the practice of putting a special garment on the baptized person; that's also something you might make. (It is generally a simple, white, poncho-like garment appropriate to the size of the person, perhaps decorated with a symbol such as a cross.) You could offer to pay for a baptismal gown, or for refreshments at a celebration after church. You might make a baptismal banner, a small one with imagery of baptism and the child's name and the date, for the child to keep. In consultation with the pastor, you could write prayers for the child, the family, and the sponsors, which would be included in the service. You could write your own prayer of blessing for your godchild, which you could say while touching her or him either during the service or at the gathering after church.

In the baptism service itself, it is important for you to say your responses so you can be heard. The portions where the godparent speaks on behalf of the child begin at the top of page 123 in *LBW*. If you have not memorized the creed (the part that begins "Do you believe in God the Father?"), make sure you will have a copy of it where you can see it, even if you will be holding something (or someone!) at the time.

Other than spoken responses during the service, there is a lot of latitude about who does what. *Lutheran Book of Worship* does not assign specific actions to a particular parent or sponsor. Find out what the customs are in this congregation, and then volunteer to do something active. When in years to come you talk to your godchild about her or his baptism, it will help make your relationship to the child concrete if you can say, "This is what I did when you were baptized!" Hold the child, either before, during, or after the baptismal washing. Pour water into the font from a pitcher during the prayer of thanksgiving (*LBW*, p.122). Make the sign of the cross on the child's head after the pastor does so (in some Hispanic congregations many people from the congregation do this). Light the baptismal candle from the paschal candle, or be the one to receive the lit candle on the child's behalf. Be one of the lectors, reading one of the biblical lessons in the service.

In consultation with the pastor, you and the other sponsors might even want to write an additional question-and-answer just for the sponsors, to supplement the question (*LBW*, p. 121) about spiritual nurture to which both parents and godparents respond. The question in *LBW* summarizes the task of raising the child in the faith, a task shared by all the adults who bring the child for baptism. An additional question for sponsors would not change that, but it could reflect the unique nature of the godparent's role.

Participating in Your Godchild's Ongoing Faith Journey

If you get a little uncomfortable when you hear words like "spiritual mentor" applied to you, you are not alone! Many of us, even as committed Christians, find it hard to imagine how we might contribute to the Christian nurture of a child who is not our own son or daughter. What should I do—ask him how he likes church? Give her a doll that says prayers? If the only religious things we can imagine doing feel uncomfortably preachy or pious, we may never develop the spiritual side of godparenting at all. And the church has not helped much. Most of the time, it has said to godparents, "Pray for your godchild, and set a good example for her or him." Fine advice, but it does not give much guidance on how to establish a relationship with your godchild. Perhaps this book can help.

Connecting With Your Godchild

Like any spiritual relationship, godparenting is nothing if it is not a genuine human relationship of appreciation and care. The guidelines for relating to a child are the same as the ones for relating to an adult. Instead of expecting children to fit into an adult world, God calls us to make room in our lives and in our hearts for the child's reality. Set aside time to do whatever the child wants to do, joining a preschooler in imaginative play or taking an older child to a movie of his choice. Listen to your godchild respectfully. Take what she says as seriously as if she were a grown-up friend. Look at her when she talks, let her finish her sentences, make comments that repeat the core of what she said so she knows you're really listening. Look for things to appreciate in your godchild, and tell him what you see.

A Long-Distance Relationship

If you live far away from your godchild, don't give up on creating a relationship. Many adults believe that they cannot be important in the life of a small child unless they see her often and spend a lot of time with her. In fact, even a two-year-old can have a relationship with a faraway adult that is important to him. Visits are helpful in making you real to a small child, but much can be done through the mail. Young children love getting mail addressed to them, and notes or cards with age-appropriate enclosures (stickers or postcards cut up into jigsaw puzzles or newspaper comics) will remind them of you and your caring. You can read or sing to the child on a tape, or make a videotape for her. You can talk on the phone; with small children, get clues from a parent first on what has been going on in the child's life, so you'll know what to ask about. For some older children, e-mail is the easiest way to communicate long-distance. If you are willing to invest the time and energy, you can make a significant relationship with a faraway child. You can find more advice on how to do this in self-help books written for long-distance grandparents.

Reminding Your Godchild of Baptism

You are a witness and a crucial participant in your godchild's baptism. A big part of your ongoing role in the child's spiritual life is to remind her that she is baptized, and to explore with her what that means. You do this simply by telling him that you are his godmother or godfather, and explaining what that means. You do it by sharing memories of the baptism day itself, perhaps with the help of photographs or a description of the day you wrote shortly after the baptism.

Another way to remind the child of her baptism is to recognize the baptismal anniversary every year. If you can be together around that time, you can gather with the child and family for a baptismal remembrance (something like a cake will make it more festive and appealing to a child), at which the baptismal candle may be lighted. Or do something water-related together: go swimming, play with boats in the bathtub, walk by the ocean or lake or river, paint with watercolors, visit an aquarium, drive through a car wash (an adventure for some children!). Make the connection that you are doing something "watery" to remember the child's baptism. If you cannot be together, send a card; make one, or get a blank card with a watery scene. Write a note saying something you remember about the baptism, and tell your godchild how much you and God both care about and love him. You might give water-related presents, too: toys for beach or bathtub, bubble-blowers, squirt toys (there are lots that are not shaped like guns), water sports equipment, or picture books of the biblical water stories (Noah's ark, the crossing of the Red Sea, the rescue of baby Moses, Jonah).

Another appropriate time to talk to your godchild about her baptism is at Easter. As Paul writes in Romans 6:3-4, the new life given in baptism has everything to do with Easter. Write your godchild a note at Easter with some mention of baptism as the gift of resurrection life. Take your godchild to one of the dramatic, late-at-night Easter services: an Easter Vigil or an Eastern Orthodox Easter midnight service. Many children will love the drama of the fire, the darkness, and the candles (not to mention staying up late!). If you emphasize Easter and baptismal day over Christmas and birthday, you've already given your relationship with your godchild a distinctively godparental character.

SHARING FAITH AND VALUES

There are countless ways in which you can share your faith with your godchild.
- "Place in their hands the Holy Scriptures" (*LBW*, p. 121). Give picture books of Bible stories, a children's Bible, or tapes or videos of Bible stories.
- Draw pictures with him about Bible stories, baptism, Christmas, or Easter.
- Let her designate some of your charitable giving.
- Play board games that allow for the discussion of feelings and values (the Ungame, LifeStories, Choices, Chatter Matters).
- Pray for him, and let him know you do so. Ask him what he would like you to say to God about him in your prayers.
- Make a bedtime tape where you sing a religious lullaby, such as "All Through the Night," "Thy holy wings" (*With One Voice* 741), or stanza 2 of "Now rest beneath night's shadow" (*LBW* 282).
- Ask her what she thinks God has to do with friendships, war, evolution, the food we eat.
- Talk to him about the names we use for God. How is God like (and not like) a father, a mother, a friend, a shepherd, a king?
- Give books that deal with religious themes (ask a children's librarian), and read them yourself, so you can talk about them together.

No one is going to be comfortable with doing all of these things. The important thing is to find ways of faith-sharing that work for the two of you, based on the child's age and both your personalities. It should feel natural, not forced, whether you are drawing together with a toddler or discussing a movie with a teen. But remember: hardly anything feels natural the first time!

When Your Godchild Becomes an Adult

Godparenthood is a lifelong relationship. If you have formed a significant relationship with your godchild during her childhood, it will feel natural to keep in touch. If you have not kept contact, it is never too late to try to reconnect! One godfather who had not seen his teenaged godson in a dozen years reached out to him on e-mail, and they developed a close relationship online. Older adolescents and adults, like children, continue to need older adults who care about them in addition to parents. Continue to share faith stories, especially stories of how your faith has changed or what has helped you in times of crisis or failure. Pay special attention to times of transition in your adult godchild's life. You might host a graduation party, write about the promise of baptism to a mourning goddaughter, give a recording of sung table graces to a godson whose baby has started eating at the table. Whether your godchild remains connected with the church or not, your continued care will be a reminder for him that the promise of God is always there for him, a witness to her that the God who raised Jesus from the dead offers her new life in every change and ending in her life. And if you find ways to share your faith and questions with each other, it is likely to be as much of a gift to you as it will be to your godchild.

Sponsoring an Adult

Even churches that have long had the practice of baptizing babies are rediscovering the importance of adult baptism, and sponsors play a crucial role in that process. The nature of the sponsor's responsibilities, of course, is somewhat different. Much of the baptismal candidate's physical and emotional maturing is done. What is often overlooked, though, is that there is much spiritual maturation that needs to take place. No matter how wise or gifted a person may be, if he or she is just entering the Christian life, it will be a growth process. Those of us who have grown up within the church tend to take for granted things like the shape of the liturgy, the practice of prayer, the habit (or struggle!) of Bible reading. For the adult going through the baptismal washing, that will all be new. And, as the Ethiopian official asked Philip, "How can I [understand], unless someone guides me?" (Acts 8:31). You, as sponsor, are one of those key "someones."

The Lutheran church, along with other denominations, is reviving the ancient process of the catechumenate. The word is a Greek term referring to the forming of a person into a mature Christian. Using resources such as the *Welcome to Christ* booklets listed in Appendix B, a congregation can bring together a wholistic ministry to help integrate new adult Christians into the local Christian community as well as the larger church.

Sponsors or godparents are key to this process. As Professor Walter Huffman has written:

In the church's catechumenal ministry the community itself sponsors catechumens [those being baptized] by offering guidance, prayer, and the witness of its own life of service to Christ. At the same time, an entire community cannot minister to an individual in the same way that one other person can. An individual sponsor embodies the Christian faith to those who are exploring the Christian faith.

Welcome to Christ: A Lutheran Introduction to the Catechumenate, p. 31

If you are being asked to be a sponsor for an adult, it is because you are recognized as one who is mature enough in faith to help another person begin the faith journey. That does not mean that you are, or need to be, the perfect Christian. All of us are both sinner and saint, and it will be helpful for the person entering baptism to see that. And you will not be alone in mentoring the new Christian. Whether the congregation is using the formal catechumenal process or not, pastors and other congregational members alike will be happy to advise you and join you in welcoming the new member into the body of Christ.

APPENDIX A / NOTES ON THE BAPTISM

You probably will receive some sort of certificate or other official remembrance of the baptism for which you are a sponsor. You may also use this page to make a record of the day, as well as follow-up that has occurred or could in the future.

Name of baptized person:

Date of baptism:

Congregation:

Pastor:

Sponsors:

Particular memories of the day and the baptism:

Ways in which the baptismal anniversary has been or could be marked:

APPENDIX B / ADDITIONAL RESOURCES

When a Child Is Being Baptized

Exploring the Sacraments with Young Children. Leader Sourcebook. Minneapolis: Augsburg Fortress, 1998.

My Place at God's Table. Child's Book and Family Book. Minneapolis: Augsburg Fortress, 1998.

A Splash of Welcome Water. Child's book. Minneapolis: Augsburg Fortress, 1998.

Welcome Water. Parent book. Minneapolis: Augsburg Fortress, 1998.

When an Adult Is Being Baptized

Access Bible (NRSV). A Bible designed especially for use with people new to the faith or to Bible study. New York: Oxford University Press, 1999.

Connections: Faith and Life. Evangelical Lutheran Church in America, Division for Congregational Ministries, 1997. Series of four participant books and leader resources for small groups based on Luther's catechisms and focused on opportunities for ministry in daily life.

Gathered and Sent: An Introduction to Worship. Participant book by Karen G. Bockelman. Leader guide by Roger Prehn. Minneapolis: Augsburg Fortress, 1999.

Lutheran Basics. Minneapolis: Augsburg Fortress, 1998.

Welcome to Christ: A Lutheran Introduction to the Catechumenate. Minneapolis: Augsburg Fortress, 1997.

Welcome to Christ: A Lutheran Catechetical Guide. Minneapolis: Augsburg Fortress, 1997.

Welcome to Christ: Lutheran Rites for the Catechumenate. Minneapolis: Augsburg Fortress, 1997.

What Do You Seek: Welcoming the Adult Inquirer. Minneapolis: Augsburg Fortress, 2000.